A Chase in the Caves

By Sally Cowan

Mint came up to Dad.

“Can I help, Dad?” said Mint.

Dad gave Mint a big job!

“Pack the grapes in crates,” said Dad.

“Then rake up the mess.”

It got hot.

Mint sat at the base
of a trunk.
She ate grapes in the shade.

Jade came to see Mint.

"Chase me!" said Mint.

But the caves all looked the same.

Mint and Jade got lost!

A blaze of sun!
Save us, Jade!

Back at home,

Dad had made a cake.

CHECKING FOR MEANING

1. What did Dad ask Mint to do? *(Literal)*
2. What did Jade want Mint to do? *(Literal)*
3. Do you think Mint enjoyed the chase in the caves? Why? *(Inferential)*

EXTENDING VOCABULARY

crates	What is a crate? What sorts of things are kept in crates?
rake	What does it mean if you are raking something? The word *rake* also means the thing used to rake. What other words can you think of that are both an action and a thing, such as *mop*?
wade	What are the sounds in the word *wade*? How many syllables are in the word? What word could the author have used instead of *wade*?

MOVING BEYOND THE TEXT

1. Bats are one type of animal that may live in caves. What other animals might live in caves?
2. What jobs or chores can you help with at home?
3. Jade and Mint like to wade in the lake, chase each other and eat grapes outside. What do you like to do outside?
4. What do you think Mint did after the story ended?

TIME TO WRITE

Write about jobs you help with around the house.

PRACTICE WORDS

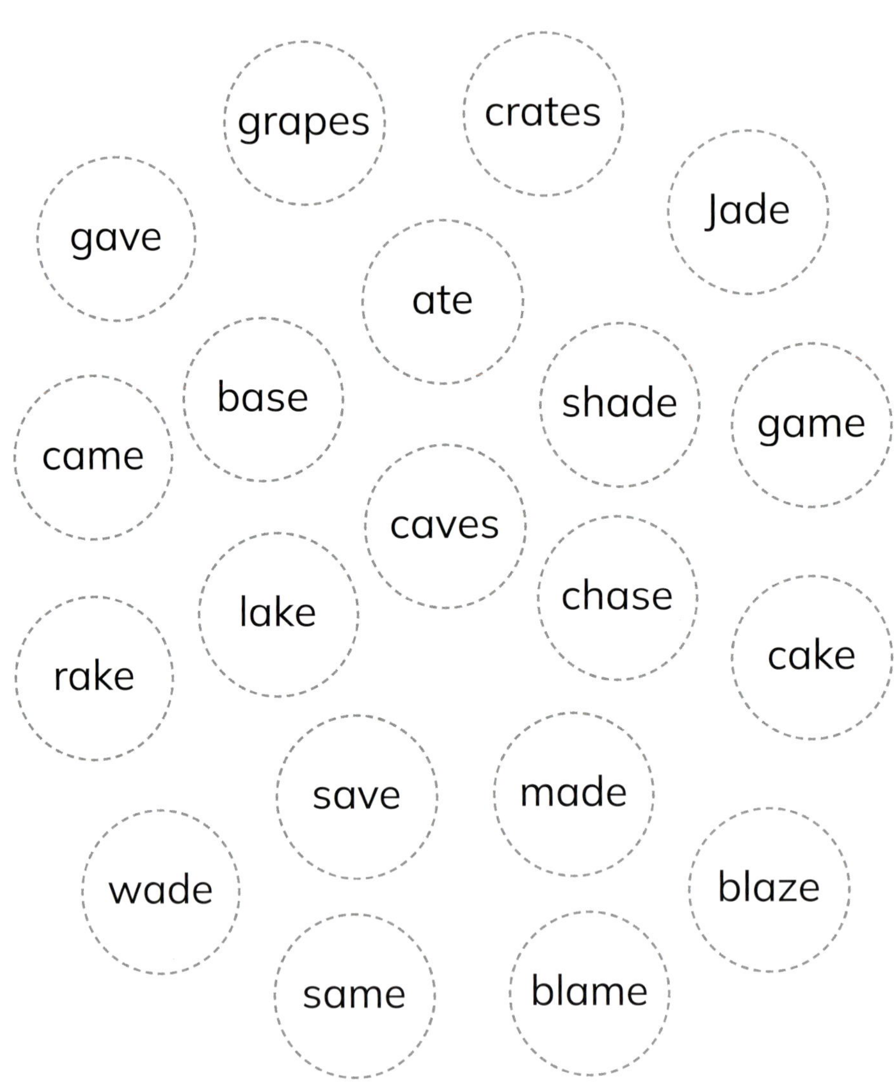